Generative AI Trends

Driving Innovation
and Business Solutions

Taylor Royce

DEDICATION

To the pioneers, inventors, and visionaries who have the courage to embrace the future and question the current quo. This book is devoted to people who believe that technology has the power to revolutionize entire sectors, resolve challenging issues, and bring about significant change. I hope the ideas and tactics presented here encourage you to take advantage of generative AI's potential and open up new avenues for development and creativity.

Your advice and support have been vital to my mentors, classmates, and coworkers who have consistently pushed the limits of knowledge. Without your assistance, this job would not have been feasible.

And lastly, this adventure is for everyone who is enthusiastic about influencing the future.

DISCLAIMER

This book's content is solely intended for informational and educational purposes. Although every attempt has been taken to guarantee the content's accuracy and completeness, the author and publisher make no guarantees or assurances about the information's completeness, accuracy, or applicability.

The author's opinions are those of the book and may not represent those of any organizations or entities with which the author has affiliations.

Before making any technological or business decisions based on the information in this book, readers are urged to do their own study and speak with experts in the field. Any losses, damages, or repercussions resulting from the use of the information in this book are not the responsibility of the author or publisher.

The owners of all trademarks, service marks, and other proprietary information mentioned in this book retain ownership of them

CONTENTS

32

ACKNOWLEDGMENTS

My sincere appreciation goes out to everyone who helped and encouraged me while I was writing this book.

I want to start by expressing my gratitude to my family and friends for their unwavering support, tolerance, and comprehension. Without your love and support, I could not have finished this journey, and your belief in me has been a continual source of inspiration.

I also want to express my gratitude to all of the mentors, coworkers, and artificial intelligence specialists who have shared their knowledge and insights with me. The substance of this book has been greatly influenced by your knowledge, and I sincerely appreciate your advice.

I would like to express my gratitude to my colleagues and fellow researchers for the thought-provoking discussions and helpful criticism that have improved my concepts and methodology. Your viewpoints have enhanced and increased the value of this work.

I want to express my gratitude to all of the readers of this book for their interest in the field of generative artificial intelligence and how it may be used to drive commercial solutions. I hope this book will be a useful guide for you as you explore the fascinating and revolutionary world of artificial intelligence.

Finally, this book is dedicated to everyone who believes that innovation and technology may bring about significant change. The real forces of advancement are your vision and enthusiasm.

Thank you.

CHAPTER 1

GENERATIVE AI'S DEVELOPMENT AND FOUNDATIONS

1.1 Comprehending Generative AI's History

A subfield of artificial intelligence called "generative AI" is dedicated to producing text, images, music, and even code. Its roots lie in the fundamental ideas of neural networks and machine learning, which sought to mimic human-like learning and thinking capacities. Examining the development of technology and the scholarly discoveries that established the groundwork for generative artificial intelligence is essential to comprehending its beginnings.

- **Early AI Systems:** In the middle of the 20th century, the first areas of AI study were logical reasoning and problem-solving. In the 1960s, programs like ELIZA mimicked human-like interactions using rule-based systems, but they

1

lacked real creative powers.

- **The Development of Neural Networks:** A move toward simulating the structure of the human brain was signaled by the development of artificial neural networks in the 1980s and 1990s. The foundation for the creation of more complex models was laid by early networks that concentrated on supervised learning, employing labeled data to generate predictions or classifications.

- **The Role of Unsupervised Learning:** The development of unsupervised learning methods, which enabled models to recognize patterns in data without explicit labels, gave generative AI a boost. This feature is essential for producing fresh, undiscovered material.

- **Generative Models' Birth:** Models such as Deep Belief Networks (DBNs) and Restricted Boltzmann Machines (RBMs) were introduced in the late 2000s. A fundamental tenet of generative artificial intelligence, these systems showed that they could produce data that looked like the training inputs.

1.2 Significant Turning Points in the Evolution of GenAI

A number of significant turning points have occurred in the development of generative AI, each signifying an advancement in both capacity and application. These developments demonstrate how generative AI progressed from abstract ideas to useful instruments with a broad range of uses.

The following is an introduction to Generative Adversarial Networks, or GANs:

Ian Goodfellow and his group unveiled GANs, a revolutionary architecture, in 2014. A discriminator and a generator are two neural networks that compete with one another to produce realistic data in GANs.

- GANs can be used for picture synthesis, video production, and producing realistic textures for simulations and video games.

Language models and transformers: Natural language processing was transformed in 2017 when Vaswani et al. unveiled the Transformer architecture. Transformers enable the creation of potent language models by using self-attention mechanisms to comprehend context over lengthy sequences.

- OpenAI's 2018 release of GPT (Generative Pre-trained Transformer) showed notable progress in text generation. Later generations, such as GPT-3 and GPT-4, demonstrated the capacity to produce text that is both contextually relevant and cohesive across a range of domains.

Image Generation and Diffusion Models: One interesting technique for producing high-quality photographs is the use of diffusion models. These models are used in media, design, and art to produce detailed images by gradually denoising random noise.

The multimodal models are as follows: Recent developments have resulted in the creation of models that can handle various kinds of data, including text-to-image systems (e.g., DALL·E, Stable Diffusion). These systems increase the creative potential of Generative AI by integrating it with various modalities.

1.3 The Differences Between Generative and Conventional AI Models

Understanding how generative AI differs from conventional AI models is crucial to appreciating its disruptive potential. Although they both use neural networks and machine learning, their goals, methods, and uses are very different.

Aim and Result:

- **Conventional AI Models**: Classification, prediction, and optimization are among the tasks that these models concentrate on. For example, they could use previous data to forecast market values or categorize spam emails.

- **Generative AI:** This technology produces original content rather than just analyzing data. It can create unique artwork, realistic voice samples, or articles that showcase human inventiveness, for instance.

Data Dependency:

- **Traditional AI:** Training primarily uses labeled datasets. The focus is on correctly recognizing or classifying the data that is currently available.

- **Generative AI:** Makes use of both labeled and unlabeled data, emphasizing the identification of patterns to generate unique results.

Model Architecture:

- **Traditional AI:** Usually employs less complex structures to address particular issues, such as feed-forward neural networks, logistic regression, or decision trees.

- In order to handle high-dimensional input and generate a variety of outputs, generative artificial intelligence (AI) uses sophisticated architectures such as GANs, transformers, and variational autoencoders (VAEs).

Applications:

- **Traditional AI:** Widely utilized in fields including medical diagnostics, recommendation systems, and fraud detection.

- The creative industries are dominated by generative artificial intelligence (AI), which makes it possible for applications like virtual reality settings, automated content generation, and customized marketing campaigns.

The development of generative AI is indicative of more general developments in computational sciences and artificial intelligence. We can gain a greater understanding of its revolutionary potential by investigating its beginnings, significant events, and distinctive features. Generative AI is a revolution in how we engage with and utilize data, creativity, and technology, not just a tool. It is a pillar of the digital age because of its capacity to combine machine precision with human-like creativity.

CHAPTER 2

GENERATIVE AI's MECHANISMS

2.1 Variational Autoencoders (VAEs) and Generative Adversarial Networks (GANs)

Two fundamental architectures in generative artificial intelligence are variational autoencoders (VAEs) and generative adversarial networks (GANs). Each takes a different approach to content creation, and comprehending their workings is essential to recognizing their functions in contemporary AI applications.

GANs (Generative Adversarial Networks)

Ian Goodfellow first presented the GAN class of machine learning models in 2014. They use two neural networks in a novel adversarial training mechanism:

The generator is as follows: In order to replicate the features of the training dataset, the generator generates new data. Image synthesis, for example, may produce realistic-looking images that seem to fall into the same category as the training photos. Its goal is to "fool" the discriminator by generating outputs that are identical to actual data.

The discriminator assesses data to determine if it is authentic (derived from the training dataset) or fraudulent (generated by the generator).

- By penalizing implausible results, it serves as a critic, assisting the generator in improving its outputs.

The generator and discriminator engage in competition throughout the Adversarial Training phase. While the discriminator becomes more adept at spotting fakes, the generator enhances its outputs to fool it. As the generator learns to provide more realistic data, this iterative process produces high-quality outputs.

GAN Applications:
- Image production and editing, including improving photo resolution or producing photorealistic images.

- Animation and synthesis of videos.

- The creation of music and audio.

- Using virtual settings to simulate real-world situations.

VAEs, or Variational Autoencoders

VAEs approach generative modeling from a probabilistic perspective. Their goal is to create new data points by learning latent representations of the data.

The encoder compresses input data into a latent space, which is represented as a probability distribution, according to the encoder-decoder framework. In order to ensure that the output data is comparable to the original input, the decoder reconstructs data from this latent representation.

An example of latent space sampling is: By learning a probability distribution in the latent space, VAEs add stochasticity in contrast to conventional autoencoders. This enables the model to sample from the learned distribution and produce fresh, varied outputs.

VAE Applications:

- Producing realistic variations of input data, including facial traits or handwriting styles.
- Finding outliers in the latent space allows for the discovery of anomalies.
- Reinforcement learning for settings that need a variety of simulations.

2.2 Large Language Models (LLMs) and Transformer Models

Generative AI has been reinterpreted by transformer models, particularly in the field of natural language processing (NLP). Powerful large language models (LLMs) have been made possible by their capacity to analyze sequential input and comprehend context.

Architecture of the Transformer

Because of its effectiveness and scalability, the Transformer architecture, which was first presented by Vaswani et al. in 2017, supplanted long short-term memory (LSTM) models and recurrent neural networks (RNNs) for a variety of tasks.

The self-attention mechanism is as follows: When producing outputs, the model can concentrate on pertinent segments of the input sequence thanks to the self-attention mechanism. For instance, the model can identify the words in a sentence that are contextually significant for comprehending a certain phrase.

Multi-Head Attention: This self-attention addition enables the model to simultaneously capture various relationship types, improving its comprehension of intricate dependencies.

Positional encodings are added to inputs to provide information about word order because transformers are not naturally capable of processing sequences.

Big Language Models (LLMs)

Transformer-based models that have been pre-trained on extensive text corpora are known as LLMs. They can be used as general-purpose generators or tailored for particular applications. Google's BERT and LaMDA, as well as OpenAI's GPT series, are examples.

In order to anticipate the next word in a sequence, LLMs are trained on large datasets, which allows them to comprehend context, idioms, and linguistic subtleties.

Fine-tuning:

- Following pretraining, models are adjusted for particular tasks, including translation, summarization, or conversational AI, or on domain-specific data.

LLMs' Capabilities:

- Producing writing that is contextually appropriate and coherent.
- Responding to inquiries, finishing phrases, or having discussions.
- Text rewriting, translation, or summarization.
- Writing programming, coming up with original content, or helping with research.

2.3 The Function of Training and Data in the Development of GenAI

Generative AI relies heavily on data and training. Model performance and accuracy are strongly impacted by the volume, quality, and diversity of data.

Data Is Important

- **Diversity:** Diverse datasets help models produce a range of outputs and improve generalization. An image generator educated on a variety of artistic styles, for instance, can successfully mimic several art forms.

- **Quality:** Accurate patterns are learned by the model when the data is of high quality. Subpar or biased outcomes might result from biased or poor data.

The labeling is as follows: A precise label is essential in supervised learning. Even unsupervised and semi-supervised methods for generative AI gain from well selected datasets.

Process of Training

- **Model Setup:** The model's weights are initialized at the start of the training phase, often using random numbers.

- **Forward Pass and Loss Calculation:** After data is run through the model, the loss function determines how much the output differs from the intended outcome.

- **Backpropagation and Optimization:** To update the model's parameters and reduce errors over time, gradients of the loss function are calculated and propagated backward.

- **Time Periods and Recurrences:** The model cycles over the complete dataset during training, which usually entails several epochs, in order to improve its comprehension.

Training Difficulties

- **Computer Resources:** Large models like LLMs require a lot of processing power to train, which is typically provided by GPUs or TPUs.

- **Overfitting:** Poor generalization can result from

models that overfit to training data. Data augmentation and regularization strategies aid in reducing this problem.

- **Bias and Ethical Considerations:** Training data can introduce biases into models. To reduce ethical issues, developers must carefully select datasets and apply strategies.

The intricacy and breadth of the field are demonstrated by the workings of generative AI. These technologies show how far Generative AI has advanced, from the adversarial dynamics of GANs and the probabilistic nature of VAEs to the revolutionary power of LLMs. Fundamentally, the extraordinary inventiveness and promise of generative AI are propelled by the combination of creative structures and reliable training procedures. Being aware of these dynamics enables us to use its power sensibly and efficiently.

CHAPTER 3

USING GENERATIVE AI TO CREATE CONTENT

3.1 Creation of Images and Videos

With previously unheard-of levels of creativity, automation, and efficiency, generative AI has completely transformed the image and video creation industries.

Generating Images

These days, a lot of people employ AI-driven picture production tools like DALL·E, MidJourney, and Stable Diffusion to produce visually appealing material. To create excellent images, these systems make use of models like Diffusion Models and Generative Adversarial Networks (GANs).

Applications:

- **Art and Design:** From textual input, AI generates visual thoughts to help artists generate original, creative artwork or aid in brainstorming.

- **Marketing and Branding:** Businesses create unique logos, ads, and visuals that are suited to their brand identities.
- **Fashion and Interior Design:** AI models enable for quick prototyping by simulating clothes and space ideas.
- Science and Healthcare: Generative AI creates synthetic data for studies or visualizes intricate biological structures.

Difficulties:

- Ethical issues such as deepfakes or deception.
- In outputs, striking a balance between originality and realism.

Generation of Videos

By giving static images temporal coherence, generative AI-generated videos elevate image synthesis to a new level.

Applications

- **Virtual Production:** AI produces lifelike backgrounds, characters, and animations, which expedites the filmmaking process.
- The user experience is improved by procedurally generated worlds and characters in the game.
- **Education and Training**: AI-generated video content supports virtual simulations or e-learning for professional training.
- Content Marketing: Tailored video advertisements made for particular target audiences or demographics.

Technological Insights:

- Realistic video frames are produced by sophisticated methods such as neural rendering and GAN-based models.
- AI-generated content and reinforcement learning are used in models such as DeepMind's AlphaStar to create interactive environments.

3.2 Generation of Text, Speech, and Music

By increasing automation and personalization, generative

AI is revolutionizing the way we produce and consume voice, music, and text.

Generation of Text

The generation of textual material has been revolutionized by Large Language Models (LLMs) such as GPT and BERT, which analyze and synthesize natural language with exceptional fluency.

Applications:

- **Creative Writing:** AI is used by authors for editing, drafting, and brainstorming. AI is capable of writing scripts, novels, and poetry in response to instructions.
- **Content Marketing:** AI creates product descriptions, blog entries, and ads based on audience preferences and brand tone.
- **Academic and Technical Writing**: Helps researchers with hypothesis generation, paper preparation, and summarization.
- "Conversational AI" refers to the use of conversational, contextual responses by AI-powered

chatbots and virtual assistants.

Difficulties:

- Steer clear of duplicate or copied content.
- Reducing bias in text produced using pre-existing datasets.

Generating Speech

Text-to-Speech (TTS) algorithms have advanced to produce voice outputs that are incredibly expressive and natural.

Applications

- **Accessibility:** TTS tools help people with visual impairments by translating text into speech.
- **Entertainment:** Character-specific voices are synthesized for video games, audiobooks, and animations.
- Artificial intelligence (AI)-generated voices improve interactive voice response (IVR) systems.

Technological Insights

- Tacotron and WaveNet are two models that synthesize realistic rhythms and intonations to attain great fidelity.

Generating Music

The creation of music has seen tremendous innovation because of generative AI technologies like Jukebox and OpenAI's MuseNet.

Applications:

- **Composing Original Scores:** AI is used by musicians and filmmakers as a source of ideas or as a foundation for their work.
- **Personalized Playlists:** AI-generated music adapts to different moods and tastes.
- **Restoration and Remastering:** AI improves or recreates vintage records for contemporary formats.
- **Education:** Students of music examine AI-generated pieces to learn about various styles.

Technological Insights:

- Models examine enormous music datasets spanning

tempos, styles, and genres.

- Harmony is ensured by methods such as sequence modeling, which forecast the subsequent note or chord.

3.3 Applications of Software Code and Product Design

With its ability to automate processes and foster creativity, generative AI is revolutionizing software development and product creation.

Generation of Software Code

The way developers write and debug code is changing as a result of AI tools like DeepCode, GitHub Copilot, and OpenAI's Codex.

Applications:

- **Automating Code Writing:** AI saves developers time by producing boilerplate code.
- **Debugging:** Tools find problems and offer solutions instantly.
- **Learning and Prototyping**: Novices use AI to

rapidly develop prototypes or comprehend coding concepts.

- **Improving Productivity:** AI manages repetitive chores while developers concentrate on logic and architecture.

Ensuring code security and quality in scripts that are created presents a challenge.

Resolving moral dilemmas, such training data plagiarism.

Applications for Product Design

In design-oriented businesses, generative AI is expanding the possibilities for efficiency and innovation.

Applications:

- **Industrial Design:** AI models provide efficient prototypes for consumer products, automobiles, and machinery.
- AI techniques help architects create ideas that are both visually beautiful and structurally sound.
- **Virtual reality and gaming:** procedurally generated objects and surroundings enhance immersive

experiences.

- **Fashion and Jewelry:** Designers experiment with unusual shapes and patterns using AI.

Technological Insights:

- Generative Design Algorithms: - These systems iteratively improve designs according to goals such as aesthetic appeal or material efficiency.
- Simulation and Feedback: AI models test designs prior to manufacturing by simulating real-world settings.

By surpassing human constraints in originality, efficiency, and customisation, generative AI in content creation has created new opportunities. Its uses are as diverse as they are revolutionary, ranging from creating captivating text, speech, and music to producing stunning images and realistic videos. Its ability to automate and innovate across industries is further highlighted by its involvement in software and product design. We may safely utilize the full potential of generative AI if we comprehend and embrace these capabilities while resolving ethical and technical issues.

CHAPTER 4

Using GenAI to Drive Business Strategy and Innovation

4.1 Use Cases in Product Development, Marketing, and Customer Support

A key component in changing corporate environments, spurring innovation, and improving operational effectiveness in marketing, product development, and customer support is generative artificial intelligence (GenAI).

Applications for Marketing

Marketing strategies are now more dynamic and individualized due to GenAI's capacity to evaluate consumer behavior, forecast trends, and provide content.

Personalized Campaigns:

- AI creates customized emails, ads, and social media posts according to the tastes and actions of each user.
- For instance, GenAI is used by an e-commerce platform to generate promotional emails and product recommendations for particular client segments.

Content Creation:

- In just a few seconds, automated systems produce eye-catching blog entries, ad copy, and visuals.
- For instance, businesses may swiftly create on-brand text and images with the help of companies like Canva and Jasper AI.

Market Insights and Trend Prediction:

- AI algorithms use extensive dataset analysis to forecast market trends and customer preferences.
- For instance, retailers may optimize marketing and inventories by using AI to predict seasonal product demand.

Product Development

Generative AI helps with ideation, design, and iteration, which speeds up innovation.

Design and Prototyping: AI creates several design iterations that mimic actual performance for assessment.

- For instance, AI is used by automakers to create models of cars that are aerodynamically efficient.

Innovative Features: AI tools help create features based on feedback and user behavior.

- For instance, software firms utilize AI to assess user interfaces and provide recommendations for enhancements based on actual usage data.

Research and Development: GenAI creates theories, synthesizes research data, and even helps create new materials.

- For instance, GenAI is used by pharmaceutical companies to model and simulate molecular structures in order to find new drugs.

Service to Customers

Real-time, effective, and customized interactions are provided by AI-powered technologies, which improve client experiences.

Chatbots and Virtual Assistants: AI chatbots such as

ChatGPT interact with users in natural language and answer their questions around-the-clock.

- For instance, airlines use AI to help with itinerary changes, flight updates, and ticket booking.

Sentiment Analysis: AI analyzes consumer reviews to spot patterns of discontent and recommend fixes.

- E-commerce platforms, for instance, use review analysis to improve their product and service offers.

Self-Service Tools: AI develops user-friendly interfaces that let users fix common problems on their own.

- For instance, financial institutions provide AI-powered solutions for updating application statuses and determining loan eligibility.

4.2 Adapting GenAI Models to Industry-Specific Problems

Although GenAI has many uses, its full potential is in industry-specific adaptation, which enables companies to successfully handle certain problems.

Personalized AI Options

By incorporating domain-specific datasets and goals, GenAI models can be optimized to meet the needs of particular businesses.

Healthcare: AI helps with patient involvement, treatment planning, and diagnosis.

- For instance, hospitals utilize AI to mine patient data for individualized health insights.

Finance: GenAI models use financial data analysis to automate reporting and forecast market trends.

- For instance, hedge funds use AI to optimize their portfolios and trade algorithmically.

Manufacturing: AI forecasts equipment maintenance requirements and optimizes production processes.

- For instance, in order to reduce downtime, factories use predictive maintenance models.

Retail: AI uses predictive analytics to improve customer experience and inventory management.

- For instance, in retail platforms, GenAI provides tailored product recommendations.

Business Ecosystem Integration

Aligning AI models with current workflows, objectives, and tools is a necessary step in customization.

Data Integration:

To guarantee accuracy and relevance, AI models are trained on proprietary datasets.

- As an illustration, a logistics company optimizes delivery routes by integrating AI with its supply chain management software.

Ethical Compliance: Tailored AI solutions follow ethical standards and industry laws.

- For instance, AI systems used in the medical industry adhere to HIPAA regulations to protect patient data.

Scalability: Customized models can be expanded to meet expanding demands and datasets.

- For instance, AI-powered customer support systems adjust to the rise in user inquiries during busy times.

Difficulties with Personalization

Customizing AI has potential, but there are drawbacks as well, including resource investment, data quality problems, and regulatory obstacles.

Resource Requirements:

Skilled staff and processing power are needed to train specialized models.

- Solution: Scalability and management are made easier by cloud-based AI services like AWS and Azure.

Data Diversity: Accurate model performance depends on ensuring unbiased and diverse datasets.

- Solution: Companies put in place reliable pipelines for data curation and preprocessing.

4.3 Using AI-Driven Innovation to Strengthen Competitive Advantage

By encouraging innovation and optimizing procedures, integrating GenAI into business plans gives organizations a major competitive advantage.

Increasing Efficiency in Operations

AI helps companies make better decisions, cut expenses,

and streamline processes.

Automation: AI manages monotonous jobs so that staff members can concentrate on strategic endeavors.

- For instance, AI speeds up financial operations by automating the processing of invoices, which lowers human error.

Data-Driven Decisions: AI technologies enable faster and more accurate decision-making by offering actionable insights.

- For instance, real-time pricing strategy adjustments are made by retailers in response to AI-analyzed variations in demand.

Developing New Goods and Services

AI enables companies to provide innovative, one-of-a-kind solutions.

Customization:

In marketplaces with intense competition, personalized experiences set brands apart.

- For instance, streaming services boost user

engagement by making content recommendations based on customer interests.

Disruptive Technologies: AI creates ground-breaking goods that upend established market standards.

- For instance, AI-powered autonomous cars are revolutionizing the transportation industry.

Developing Client Loyalty

By providing value through tailored interactions and solutions, artificial intelligence improves client connections.

Engagement: AI helps companies to have meaningful, ongoing conversations with their clients.

- AI-powered loyalty programs, for instance, improve user retention by providing personalized rewards.

Feedback Utilization: AI uses user feedback to iteratively improve goods and services.

- For instance, AI-powered feedback mechanisms are used by mobile apps to enhance user experience.

Businesses may now thrive in marketing, product

development, and customer service because of generative AI, which is changing company innovation and strategy. Businesses can access unmatched growth prospects by tailoring AI models to industry-specific requirements and using them to boost competitive advantage. However, careful integration, moral behavior, and ongoing innovation are necessary to fully realize GenAI's promise. Businesses may take the lead in an AI-driven economy by adopting these principles and providing value to stakeholders and customers alike.

CHAPTER 5

AI LITERACY AND SELF-SERVICE INITIATIVES

5.1 Increasing Knowledge and Awareness Among Teams

Any organization's ability to successfully integrate AI is largely dependent on the knowledge and proficiency of its employees as a whole. Increasing team understanding and expertise in AI is essential to developing an innovative and flexible culture.

The Significance of Awareness

Employees who are intimidated by new technology or who are uninformed of its potential frequently oppose AI-driven products and procedures. Initiatives to raise awareness tackle these issues by:

Dispelling Myths:

Teams become less skeptical and fearful when they are informed about what AI can and cannot achieve.

- One way to reduce worry is to make it clear that AI is a tool to supplement human labor, not to replace it.

Cultivating Curiosity: Emphasizing AI's potential inspires groups to investigate innovative uses.

- As an illustration, a marketing team discovers how AI may maximize ad placements, inspiring creative approaches.

Promoting Cooperation: Awareness campaigns allow departments to coordinate on AI projects.

Methods for Acquiring Knowledge about AI

In order to teach teams effectively, firms should use customized strategies:

To clarify topics and illustrate use cases, regularly host events conducted by AI professionals through workshops and seminars.

- For instance, a session on AI-powered inventory management is held by an online retailer.

Interactive Learning Platforms: Make AI topics

interesting and approachable by using gamified learning platforms.

- For instance, staff members take part in an app that teaches the fundamentals of machine learning through quizzes.

Use Case Showcases: To encourage adoption, demonstrate practical AI applications inside the company.

- Give examples of how AI has improved customer service metrics.

5.2 Creating Successful AI Literacy Programs

Programs for AI literacy that work are organized, inclusive, and centered on giving staff members the confidence to use AI.

The Fundamentals of AI Literacy

A successful program encompasses a variety of competences, ranging from fundamental information to sophisticated abilities:

Comprehending AI Fundamentals:

Subjects covered include generative AI, machine learning, and natural language processing.

- For instance, staff members are taught how AI algorithms on e-commerce platforms suggest things.

Assuring ethical alignment requires talking about biases, data privacy, and responsible AI use.

- As an illustration, groups examine case studies of biased AI models and talk about potential fixes.

Hands-on Training: Giving staff members access to AI platforms and tools encourages practice and creativity.

- For instance, a customer service team receives training on creating chatbots powered by AI.

How to Create Programs for AI Literacy

1. Evaluate Training Needs: Determine areas where teams' comprehension of AI is lacking.

- For instance, administer questionnaires to determine knowledge of AI principles and resources.

2. Tailor Content to Roles: Create modules that are pertinent to particular job functions.

- For instance, while IT teams concentrate on model implementation, sales teams study AI-driven lead scoring.

3. Incorporate Blended Learning: Mix live sessions, online courses, and practical projects.

- For instance, after finishing an online course on AI ethics, staff members participate in a team hackathon.

4. Involve External Experts: Collaborate with AI experts to get state-of-the-art information and resources.

- For instance, work with academic institutions that provide AI certification courses.

Promoting a Lifelong Learning Culture

AI literacy should be a continuous process rather than a one-time event:

Continuous Updates:

Update content frequently to take advantage of AI developments.

- For instance, provide fresh lessons on generative AI programs like DALL-E or ChatGPT.

Promote Peer Learning: Establish channels for staff members to exchange AI best practices and use cases.

- An example might be internal forums where staff members talk about AI tools they've successfully used.

5.3 Assessing AI Literacy Programs' Effects

AI literacy initiatives are certain to provide value and stay in line with corporate objectives when their effectiveness is measured.

Evaluation Key Metrics

Organizations should monitor both qualitative and quantitative measures in order to assess the impact of their programs:

Employee Engagement: Track training session comments and participation rates.
- For instance, track survey satisfaction levels and online AI module completion rates.

Skill Acquisition: Evaluate staff members' proficiency with AI concepts and tools in their positions.
- Test your ability to use AI-driven analytics

applications, for instance.

Business Outcomes: Connect AI literacy to quantifiable increases in creativity and productivity.

- For instance, monitor revenue growth attributable to AI-optimized advertising campaigns.

Putting Feedback Loops in Place

Programs for AI literacy are improved by feedback mechanisms:

Participant feedback on the relevance of the content and delivery strategies is gathered through surveys and interviews.

- For instance, survey participants after training to find any gaps or areas that need work.

Performance tracking: Track how key performance indicators (KPIs) have changed following training.

- Examine whether AI-driven project timelines improved after training, for instance.

Iterative Updates: Apply insights to continuously enhance the structure and content of the program.

Evaluation of Long-Term Impact

Over time, organizations should assess the wider impacts of AI literacy initiatives:

Cultural Shift:
Assess how corporate perspectives on AI have changed.

- For instance, a rise in employee-led AI application concepts suggests a change in culture.

Cross-Functional Collaboration: Evaluate how departmental collaboration is facilitated by AI literacy.

- For instance, after training, the number of joint projects between the data science and marketing teams increases.

Innovation Metrics: Monitor the quantity of patents and innovations produced by teams using AI.

Programs for self-service and AI literacy are essential to ensuring that businesses fully utilize AI technologies. Businesses may enable staff members to smoothly incorporate AI into their jobs by raising awareness, creating strong literacy programs, and tracking their results. In addition to improving individual competency, this fosters organizational expansion, creativity, and a competitive advantage in an AI-driven market.

CHAPTER 6

METHODICAL TECHNIQUES FOR DEVELOPING USE CASES AND GENERATING IDEAS

6.1 Putting AI Solutions in a Constant Feedback Loop

Keeping an ongoing feedback loop is one of the fundamentals of a successful AI deployment. By integrating feedback from stakeholders and end users, this iterative method guarantees that AI solutions continue to be accurate, useful, and relevant over time.

The Significance of Feedback Loops

- **Adaptability:** AI systems need to be able to adjust to shifting user habits, data patterns, and business settings. Feedback loops increase the accuracy of decisions and aid in model refinement.
- **User-Centric Improvement:** Organizations can pinpoint issues and enhance AI systems for

improved usability and functionality by incorporating user feedback.

- **Performance Monitoring:** Feedback loops offer a way to keep an eye on how well the system is working in actual situations, making sure that it is in line with the desired objectives.

Creating a Successful Feedback Loop

1. Data Collection Points: Put in place mechanisms to gather input at different points of contact.

- Use customer satisfaction surveys after interacting with an AI chatbot, for instance.

2. Integration of Feedback: Retrain models, upgrade functionality, and address errors using the feedback.

- As an illustration, use user input to improve a recommendation engine's algorithm.

3. Regular Updates: Plan iterative updates according to insights and data gathered.

- An AI-driven pricing tool that is updated quarterly to reflect market developments is one example.

4. Stakeholder Engagement: Include all pertinent parties in the feedback process, including as developers, business executives, and end users.

- For instance, holding frequent stakeholder meetings to talk about AI performance indicators and enhancements.

Difficulties and Strategies for Mitigation

- **Overwhelming input Volume:** Use AI-driven analytics technologies to prioritize useful input.
- **Opposition to Change:** Inform interested parties of the benefits of iterative enhancements.
- **Integration Complexity:** Create efficient procedures to integrate feedback into pipelines for AI development.

6.2 Methods for Gathering and Sorting AI Use Cases

Maximizing the return on AI investments requires first identifying and ranking the most significant use cases. In order to concentrate resources on high-value projects, this calls for methodical gathering strategies and evaluation standards.

Methods to Gather Use Cases

1. To create ideas for AI use cases, arrange collaborative sessions with cross-functional teams through Brainstorming Workshops.

- For instance, consider possible AI uses in a logistics industry, like inventory forecasting or route optimization.

2. Data-Driven Insights: Examine organizational data to identify areas where AI might improve results or generate efficiency.

- For instance, examining call center transcripts to find trends for customer service driven by AI.

3. Customer Feedback: Get information from clients regarding their problems and ideal fixes.

- Example: AI-driven feature enhancements are sparked by customer suggestions for product improvements.

4. Industry Benchmarks: Examine rivals and market leaders to find AI applications that have been shown to work.

- Seeing how e-commerce behemoths employ AI for tailored advertising is one example.

Granting AI Use Cases Priority

Organizations must rank use cases according to their impact, viability, and alignment with corporate objectives after gathering suggestions.

Impact Analysis: Assess each use case's possible advantages, such as increased revenue, cost savings, or improved customer satisfaction.

- A sales forecasting tool that has the potential to yield a substantial return on investment is given a higher ranking.

Feasibility Assessment: Evaluate the necessary resources, data availability, and technical complexity.

- As an illustration, a use case that necessitates a large

amount of tagged data is deprioritized because of resource constraints.

Strategic Alignment: Verify that use cases complement the organization's overall objectives.

- As an illustration, a business that prioritizes sustainability gives AI models top priority for energy efficiency.

Prioritization Tools

Utilize scoring matrices, such as the Eisenhower Matrix, to order use cases according to their significance and urgency.

- **Cost-Benefit Analysis:** Calculate the predicted benefits for each use case in relation to the possible expenses.
- **Prototyping:** Prior to full-scale implementation, create inexpensive prototypes to confirm viability and impact.

6.3 Establishing Iterative and Dynamic Development Procedures

Rarely is AI development a one-time endeavor. A dynamic and iterative approach is necessary for successful implementation in order to account for ongoing learning, changing goals, and technology breakthroughs.

Important Iterative Development Components

1. Agile Methodologies: Use agile techniques to facilitate quick iterations and adaptability.

- For instance, create and test AI models in brief sprints using Scrum frameworks.

2. Incremental Development: Begin with an MVP and gradually add features in response to user input.

- As an illustration, start with a simple AI chatbot and gradually improve it by adding natural language comprehension.

3. Continuous Integration and Deployment (CI/CD): To guarantee smooth updates, automate testing, integration, and deployment.

- Use CI/CD pipelines, for instance, to release updated AI models without interfering with services.

4. Monitoring and Optimization: Keep an eye on AI systems in use to identify problems and enhance efficiency.

- For instance, compare new model variants using A/B testing and choose the one that performs the best.

Iterative Processes' Advantages

- **Risk Reduction:** Frequent upgrades reduce the possibility of major malfunctions.
- **Faster Time-to-Market:** Functional prototypes can be delivered more quickly thanks to iterative techniques.
- Cross-functional teams remain involved throughout the development cycle, which results in Enhanced Collaboration.

Iterative AI Development Best Practices

- **Unambiguous Goals:** Establish objectives and success criteria for every iteration.
- **Stakeholder Communication:** Keep stakeholders informed about developments and difficulties.

- **Scalable Infrastructure:** For scalable deployments, use containerization and cloud platforms.

Effective AI strategy is based on methodical approaches to use case creation and concept generating. Organizations can fully utilize AI by adopting dynamic development processes, implementing methodical methods for identifying use cases, and developing strong feedback loops. These procedures not only encourage creativity but also guarantee that, in a constantly shifting environment, AI solutions continue to be in line with user requirements and corporate objectives.

CHAPTER 7

RESPONSIBLE AI DEVELOPMENT AND ETHICAL CONSIDERATIONS

Although generative AI has enormous creative potential, there are also moral dilemmas that need to be carefully considered. The fundamentals of ethical AI are examined in this chapter, with an emphasis on reducing bias, maintaining transparency, and putting ethical standards into practice to promote responsible research and use.

7.1 Handling Generative AI Model Bias

AI model bias is still a serious problem that might support inequality and discrimination. Unexpected or unethical outcomes might result from generative AI systems that are trained on biased data since they often produce outputs that mirror or even magnify those biases.

Comprehending AI Bias

AI bias originates from a number of factors, including:

- **Historical Data:** AI results will replicate trends if the training dataset depicts current societal injustices.

- **Selection Bias:** Incomplete or skewed datasets do not accurately reflect a range of viewpoints or demographics.

- **Algorithmic Bias:** Unintentional preferences may be introduced by design choices like feature selection or weighting.

Implications of Prejudice in Generative AI

Social Impacts: Stereotypes can be reinforced by biased models, which can be detrimental to society.

- **As an illustration,** consider a generative text model that generates stereotyped descriptions according to race or gender.

Bias has the potential to erode trust and harm a brand's reputation.

- One AI-powered hiring tool that favors male applicants based on past hiring data is one example.

Legal Implications: Discriminatory results may be in violation of anti-discrimination legislation or regulations such as the GDPR.

Methods to Reduce Bias

1. Diverse and Representative Datasets: Use a variety of data sources to capture a broad spectrum of viewpoints.

- Audit datasets frequently to look for errors or unbalanced representation.

2. Bias Detection Tools: Use frameworks and algorithms to identify and measure bias in model training.

- Make use of open-source resources such as Google's What-If Tool or IBM AI Fairness 360.

3. Ongoing Monitoring: Track model performance after deployment to spot and correct any new biases.

4. Inclusive Development Teams: In order to find blind spots, involve a variety of stakeholders in the development process.

5. Iterative Training and Refinement: Retrain models using new datasets over time to lessen lingering biases.

7.2 Providing Explainability and Transparency

As generative AI systems become more intricate, maintaining explainability and transparency is critical to fostering stakeholder and user trust.

Why Openness Is Important

- **Accountability:** Developers can identify and fix mistakes in transparent systems.
- **Trust:** Intelligible AI technologies are more likely to be adopted by users.
- **Regulatory Compliance**: New legislation, such as the EU's AI Act, requires AI systems to be transparent.

Generative AI Explainability

Making AI results and decision-making processes intelligible to humans is known as explainability. Models of generative AI, like GPT or GANs, frequently operate as "black boxes," with their inner workings hidden from view.

Methods to Improve Explainability

1. Interpretable Models: Whenever feasible, use more straightforward, understandable procedures.

- For simpler jobs, decision trees or rule-based systems are examples.

2. Post-Hoc Explainability Tools: Use tools that examine outputs following their generation by the model.

- To emphasize important aspects, use SHAP (SHapley Additive exPlanations) as an example.

3. Documentation and Model Cards: Give thorough explanations of the model's goals, constraints, and training information.

- Google's Model Cards, for instance, standardize transparency procedures.

4. Visualizing Outputs: Produce visual aids to assist consumers in comprehending how the model makes decisions.

- For instance, picture generating models can display areas of interest using heatmaps.

5.   Collaboration   with   Stakeholders: Involve non-technical stakeholders to confirm the explainability and usefulness of the system.

7.3 Creating Standards for the Use of Ethical AI

Generative AI technologies are implemented ethically and in accordance with social norms when explicit criteria for ethical AI development are established.

Ethical AI Fundamentals

1. **Fairness:** AI systems ought to avoid discrimination and treat every user equally.
2. **Privacy:** User information must be safeguarded and utilized only with express permission.
3. **Accountability:** Developers ought to be held accountable for the results of AI.
4. **Safety:** AI systems need to be built with the

protection of people and society in mind.

5. **Inclusivity:** Different groups and viewpoints should be accommodated by generative AI.

How to Create Ethical AI Policies

1. Establish fundamental values and concepts that complement organizational goals by defining ethical goals.

- An AI healthcare system that puts patient safety and data privacy first is an example.

2. Create an AI Ethics Committee: Assemble a multidisciplinary group to supervise moral issues.

- Incorporate community representatives, domain specialists, and ethicists.

3. Create Ethical Policies: Draft guidelines that address important ethical issues such user consent and data usage.

4. Perform Ethical Impact Assessments: Prior to deployment, consider possible societal and environmental effects.

5. Promote Transparency: To foster trust, distribute impact analyses and ethical guidelines to stakeholders.

6. Implement Regular Audits: Arrange for recurring audits to guarantee continued adherence to moral principles.

Difficulties in Applying Ethical AI

- **Balancing Innovation and Regulation:** While too much regulation might hinder innovation, too little regulation can lead to immoral consequences.
- **Global Variability:** Regional variations in ethical standards necessitate flexible guidelines.
- **Resource Constraints:** Small businesses might not have the funds to put in place thorough ethical initiatives.

In order to create and implement generative AI responsibly, ethical issues are essential. Transparency builds trust, addressing bias guarantees justice, and clearly defined ethical standards protect social ideals. Organizations may produce innovative, inclusive, egalitarian, and socially responsible technologies by incorporating these ideas into every phase of AI development.

CHAPTER 8

SCALING GENAI THROUGHOUT THE COMPANY

Organizations have both special possibilities and problems in expanding Generative AI (GenAI) solutions as they transition from experimental use cases to essential parts of business strategy. The intricacies of scaling GenAI are explored in this chapter, along with typical problems, the significance of strong infrastructure and resource allocation, and lessons discovered from successful deployments.

8.1 Overcoming Obstacles to AI Solution Scaling

Moving from prototypes to fully integrated, enterprise-wide applications is a necessary step in scaling GenAI technologies. But there are challenges associated with this shift.

Typical Obstacles in GenAI Scaling

1. Data Limitations: Scaling requires access to broad, clean, and high-quality datasets.

- Inconsistent formats, isolated data systems, or inadequate volume are the causes of problems.

2. Model Generalization: Models created for particular activities could find it difficult to adjust to more general organizational requirements.

- It takes more knowledge and resources to fine-tune models for various departments or geographical areas.

3. Skill Gaps: A staff skilled in data science, model deployment, and AI technologies is necessary to scale GenAI.

- The skills required to properly grow and maintain these systems are lacking in many firms.

4. Cost Management: GenAI model deployment and training, especially large-scale models, can require a lot of resources.

- Data storage, cloud computing, and operational

inefficiencies can all result in unforeseen expenses.

5. The fear of obsolescence or a lack of knowledge may cause teams to be resistant to implementing AI-driven procedures.

- Successful scaling requires addressing cultural inertia.

Methods to Get Past Obstacles

- **Set Clear Objectives:** To guarantee alignment with company strategy, define precise, quantifiable goals for GenAI scaling.
- **Invest in Education and Training**: Create AI literacy initiatives to empower staff members at all levels.
- Adopting an agile approach will enable teams to adjust and provide opportunity for iterative improvements when GenAI is implemented gradually.
- **Promote Interdepartmental Cooperation**: Develop a collaborative culture to integrate data sources and match GenAI projects with business

requirements.

- Leverage Partnerships: To solve technological difficulties and talent gaps, work with other specialists like AI suppliers or educational institutions.

8.2 Allocation of Infrastructure and Resources for GenAI

A strong infrastructure is essential for a GenAI deployment to be successful. Careful planning is necessary for scaling in terms of human resources, data management, and processing capacity.

Important Infrastructure Elements for GenAI Scaling

1. Computing Power: Generative models that demand a lot of computational power, such as GPT and DALL·E, are resource-intensive.

Choices consist of:

- For the majority of businesses, cloud-based solutions are flexible, scalable, and affordable.
- **On-Premises Infrastructure:** Perfect for sectors

like finance and healthcare that have stringent data security regulations.

2. Data Storage and Management: GenAI scalability depends on effectively storing and retrieving massive datasets.

- Among the things to take into account are data lakes for unstructured data.
- Data repositories for organized analysis.
- Data streaming in real time for dynamic applications.

3. Development and Deployment Pipelines: Efficiency and consistency are guaranteed by automating the model training, testing, and deployment cycle.

- These procedures can be streamlined with the use of tools like MLflow or Kubeflow.

4. Security and Compliance: Verify that data protection procedures comply with regulatory mandates such as GDPR or HIPAA.

- To protect sensitive data, use encryption, access limitations, and frequent audits.

Assigning Resources for Scalability

- **Financial Resources:** Set aside money for cloud services, software, hardware, and continuing model upkeep.
- **Human Resources:** To close skill shortages, strike a balance between external collaborations and internal team growth.
- In order to guarantee long-term success, allot enough time for testing, improvement, and scalability.

Optimal Techniques for Resource Administration

- To prioritize investments, do a cost-benefit analysis.
- Measure ROI and support additional resource allocation with performance data.
- Establish a centralized AI governance team to manage resource allocation and scaling initiatives.

8.3 Examples of Effective GenAI Scale Implementation

Analyzing actual cases offers insightful information about

how businesses have successfully grown GenAI to spur innovation and accomplish strategic goals.

Case Study 1: GenAI in Retail

- Company: A leading global e-commerce company.
- **Application:** Tailored client interactions.

Problem: In order to increase sales and boost customer happiness, the business aimed to strengthen its recommendation engine.

- A transformer-based language model was put into place to examine user preferences and behavior.
- Utilizing generative capabilities, dynamic product descriptions customized for each buyer were produced.
- A 20% rise in click-through rates is the outcome.
- A notable increase in client retention as a result of highly customized purchasing experiences.

Case Study 2: GenAI in Healthcare

- **Business:** An international healthcare organization.
- **Application:** Analysis of medical imaging.

Problem: As the need for diagnostic imaging increased, the organization encountered a bottleneck in radiology departments.

- The use of GANs to improve image resolution and accuracy for early diagnosis is the solution.
- Explainable AI was used to give radiologists useful information.

Result:

- A 30% reduction in diagnosis time.
- Enhanced patient outcomes as a result of quicker and more precise anomaly detection.

Case study 3, "GenAI in Finance," focuses on a prominent investment firm.

- **Application**: Fraud detection and risk assessment.

Problems: The company had to minimize false positives while simultaneously detecting possible fraudulent activity in real-time.

- To identify irregularities in transaction patterns, a variational autoencoder was trained.
- To increase accuracy, generative insights were combined with conventional models.

Result:

- A 40% increase in fraud detection rates.

- Decreased operating expenses related to manually looking into transactions that have been identified.

The process of scaling generative AI throughout an enterprise is complex and calls for resolving technical issues, constructing reliable infrastructure, and taking note of successful deployments. Businesses can fully utilize GenAI to spur innovation, boost productivity, and obtain a competitive edge in a world increasingly powered by AI by using a strategic approach to scaling.

CHAPTER 9

GENERATIVE AI'S FUTURE TRENDS

Generative AI (GenAI) has rapidly progressed from a specialized field of study to a force that is revolutionizing numerous sectors. As new technologies push the limits of what these systems can accomplish, its potential keeps expanding. The significance of multimodal AI models, upcoming technologies, and projections for the next stage of development are all covered in this chapter's exploration of future developments in GenAI.

9.1 New Technologies and GenAI Developments

Significant advances in GenAI are being driven by the quick speed of technical improvement. New developments portend a fascinating future in which AI systems grow in strength, effectiveness, and accessibility.

GenAI and Quantum Computing

GenAI will be able to handle large datasets and train intricate models with previously unheard-of efficiency because of the exponential gains in processing power promised by quantum computing.

Among the possible advantages are:

- Quicker model training periods.
- Better optimization techniques that provide more complex results.

Edge AI Integration

While cloud-based infrastructure is a major component of traditional GenAI models, the trend toward edge AI is altering this dynamic.

- By allowing generative models to run directly on nearby devices, edge AI lowers latency and improves data privacy.

Real-time language translation on mobile devices is one example of an application.

- Wearable technology that generates personalized content.

Neural Architecture Advancements

The performance of GenAI models is being optimized via

innovations such as sparse transformers and effective attention methods.

- These advancements make it possible to: - Lower computational expenses.
- Enhanced scalability without compromising the accuracy of the model.

IoT and Robotics Integration

GenAI, Internet of Things (IoT) devices, and robotics are combining to open up new automation and interaction possibilities.

- Creating dynamic conversational interfaces for smart home appliances is one example.
- Enabling robots to develop context-aware and adaptive solutions for industry or medical applications.

9.2 Multimodal AI Models' Effects

The future of generative AI systems is being shaped by multimodal AI, which combines information from multiple input formats, including text, images, audio, and video. These models are expected to improve adaptability and practicality.

What Are Multimodal AI Models?

Multimodal models are capable of processing and producing content in many formats at once, in contrast to conventional single-modal systems.

- For instance, given a text instruction, a multimodal AI could produce a video with background music and subtitles.

Multimodal GenAI Applications

1. Content Creation

- Developing comprehensive multimedia campaigns that skillfully blend text, audio, and images.
- By creating scripts, images, and soundtracks from unprocessed input data, video editing can be automated.

2. Healthcare Innovations

- Helping physicians by integrating patient histories (text data) with diagnostic imaging (visual data) for thorough analysis.
- Creating   instructional   resources   that   are

patient-friendly by utilizing multimodal inputs.

3. Education and Training

- Developing virtual worlds with artificial intelligence to create immersive learning experiences.

- Creating specialized instructional materials that incorporate written summaries, interactive tests, and video lectures.

Advantages of Multimodal GenAI

- **Improved Contextual Understanding**: These systems are able to produce more precise and contextually aware outputs since they can examine many kinds of data.

- **Greater Accessibility:** AI becomes more inclusive and approachable when multimodal systems are able to accommodate a range of user preferences.

9.3 Forecasting the Upcoming Stage of GenAI Research

The next stage of generative AI research will probably concentrate on improving capabilities, resolving ethical issues, and extending its influence into new fields as it develops further.

Hyper-Personalization

By utilizing user-specific data, future GenAI systems will offer hyper-personalized experiences.

Examples of applications

- Health plans that are tailored to a person's genetic information and medical history.
- Customized marketing plans that change based on user activity in real time.

AI Systems for Collaboration

GenAI will no longer operate as stand-alone tools but rather as a component of cooperative ecosystems in which several AI systems work together to address challenging issues.

- For instance, AI models may work together in manufacturing to independently create, test, and improve goods.

AI-Generated innovation

GenAI has the potential to co-create in domains that have historically relied on human innovation, like:

- In both literature and film, plots, characters, and scripts are developed in collaboration with human creators.
- **Fine arts:** Producing unique works that skillfully combine AI and human involvement.

Regulation and Ethics

Strong ethical frameworks and regulatory requirements will be necessary as GenAI grows.

- Preventing the misuse of deepfake technology is one of the main areas of focus.
- Making sure AI-generated material is transparent.
- Preserving the rights of creators to their intellectual property.

Universal Accessibility

The goal is to make GenAI available to people, nonprofit organizations, and smaller enterprises.

- Open-source projects and cloud-based platforms will be essential to democratizing GenAI capabilities.

Complementing Emerging Domains

As blockchain, virtual reality, and augmented reality (AR)

develop, they will work in tandem with GenAI to produce ground-breaking applications.

Enabling example:

- Blockchain technology enables safe and authentic ownership of AI-generated material.

- Adding dynamic, AI-generated interactions to VR environments to improve them.

Generative AI's future is characterized by ongoing innovation and growing possibilities. AI's potential will be expanded by new technologies, multimodal capabilities, and innovative development methodologies. Unlocking AI's full potential will need a dedication to ethical and inclusive AI policies as businesses and researchers traverse this revolutionary era.

CHAPTER 10

A ROADMAP FOR USING GENAI IN YOUR ORGANIZATION IS PROVIDED

A strategic approach is necessary for the successful integration of Generative AI (GenAI) into your company. This chapter provides businesses with a clear road map for evaluating their preparedness, creating successful adoption plans, and guaranteeing ongoing development via observation and improvement.

10.1 Evaluating Organizational GenAI Readiness

Prior to using GenAI, enterprises need to assess their readiness to embrace and maintain these cutting-edge technologies. This stage guarantees that infrastructure, culture, and resources meet GenAI criteria.

1. Examine Current Infrastructure

- **Technology Stack:** Determine if your current

systems are capable of handling the math required by GenAI models.

- Does your company have access to cloud services or high-performance computing for deployment and training?
- Are systems for storing data safe, scalable, and able to manage the enormous datasets needed by GenAI?
- Readiness of Data: Analyze the quantity, quality, and diversity of the data that is available.
- Is your data sufficiently diverse, clean, and labeled to support the development of strong models?
- Is your company in compliance with data privacy laws like HIPAA or GDPR?

2. Recognize Workforce Skills

Evaluate the abilities and expertise of your group:

- Are there machine learning engineers, data scientists, or AI professionals on your team?
- Are there initiatives to upskill staff members in AI-related concepts?
- Assess the organization's capacity for change and readiness to include workflows powered by AI.

3. Examine the needs and goals of the business.

Determine the following areas where GenAI can be really beneficial:

- Improving client experiences by customizing them.
- Repetitive tasks can be automated to increase productivity.
- Promoting creativity in the creation of new products.
- To guarantee strategic alignment, match GenAI application cases with broader corporate objectives.

10.2 Developing an Adoption Strategy for GenAI

The next stage after determining preparedness is to develop a thorough plan for implementing GenAI. A well-designed strategy reduces risks, optimizes returns on investment, and offers a clear deployment roadmap.

1. Clearly define your goals and use cases

- Set quantifiable, precise objectives for the application of GenAI. Using AI-driven automation to cut operating costs by 15% is one example.
- Personalized recommendations have been shown to increase client retention rates.

- Sort use cases according to their feasibility: Can the project be completed with the resources at hand?
- Impact: What possible value addition or return on investment exists?
- Is there anything urgent that GenAI can take care of right now?

2. Create a Plan for Phased Implementation

- To examine the effects of GenAI and obtain information, start small with experimental projects.
- Successful pilots should be scaled across departments with proper training and support.
- Establish implementation schedules, resource allocation plans, and progress indicators.

3. Establish a Cooperative Environment

- Encourage cooperation between company executives, technical teams, and outside partners:
- The development and improvement of models should be the main emphasis of technical teams.
- Business executives need to match organizational strategy with AI projects.
- Collaborating with GenAI consultants or vendors

can yield invaluable knowledge.

- Promote the identification and resolution of possible obstacles by cross-functional teams.

4. Assure Responsible and Ethical Execution

Make sure the adoption strategy takes ethics into account:

- Diversifying training datasets helps prevent bias in AI models.
- Make AI decision-making procedures transparent.
- Establish a governance structure to supervise the prudent application of GenAI.

10.3 Prolonged Monitoring and Improvement of AI Solutions

The application of GenAI is not the end of the adventure. For AI systems to remain relevant and effective, organizations must constantly assess performance and make necessary adjustments.

1. Establish Performance Measures

Set up Key Performance Indicators (KPIs) to monitor how GenAI affects corporate goals.

For instance, keep an eye on measures like:

- Efficiency gains (savings of time or money).
- The precision and dependability of the thoughts or content produced.
- Scores of customer satisfaction after integrating AI.
- To see these metrics in real time, use dashboards or analytics software.

2. Perform Continual Audits

Conduct reviews on a regular basis to assess:

- Model precision and applicability: Are models evolving to meet evolving business requirements?
- The integrity of data: Does the data being used remain compliant, accurate, and relevant?
- Determine which parts of the system might need to be updated or retrained.

3. Get input from stakeholders.

Engage partners, consumers, and staff in the feedback loop:

- Workers might draw attention to difficulties when utilizing AI-powered tools.
- Consumers are able to comment on the level of personalization and quality of AI interactions.

Utilize this input to improve and hone GenAI solutions.

4. Make plans for upgrades and scalability. Make sure AI systems can expand with your company as it does.

- In order to meet the growing demand, upgrade the processing resources.
- To remain competitive, take advantage of new developments in GenAI technology.
- Review AI use cases frequently to find fresh chances to add value.

5. Take into Account Changing Ethical Issues

- Keep abreast with the laws and ethical standards pertaining to the usage of AI.
- Modify AI governance guidelines to handle emerging issues such preventing the exploitation of generative models for disinformation.
- Making sure AI decision-making remains transparent and equitable.

GenAI implementation is a continual process of innovation, ethical responsibility, and progress rather than a one-time event. Organizations may fully utilize GenAI to boost productivity, growth, and competitive advantage by evaluating preparedness, developing a solid plan, and staying dedicated to ongoing monitoring and improvement. A successful and long-lasting integration of GenAI into your company ecosystem is guaranteed if you follow this strategy.

ABOUT THE AUTHOR

 Author and thought leader in the IT field Taylor Royce is well known. He has a two-decade career and is an expert at tech trend analysis and forecasting, which enables a wide audience to understand complicated concepts.

Royce's considerable involvement in the IT industry stemmed from his passion with technology, which he developed during his computer science studies. He has extensive knowledge of the industry because of his experience in both software development and strategic consulting.

Known for his research and lucidity, he has written multiple best-selling books and contributed to esteemed tech periodicals. Translations of Royce's books throughout the world demonstrate his impact.

Royce is a well-known authority on emerging technologies and their effects on society, frequently requested as a speaker at international conferences and as a guest on tech podcasts. He promotes the development of ethical technology, emphasizing problems like data privacy and the digital divide.

In addition, with a focus on sustainable industry growth, Royce mentors upcoming tech experts and supports IT education projects. Taylor Royce is well known for his ability to combine analytical thinking with technical know-how. He sees a time when technology will ethically benefit humanity.

www.ingramcontent.com/pod-product-compliance
Lightning Source LLC
LaVergne TN
LVHW022355060326
832902LV00022B/4456